LINCOLNWOOD PUBLIC LIBRARY

3 1242 00245 0485

 W9-BEU-215

Lincolnwood Library
4000 W. Pratt Ave.
Lincolnwood, IL 60712

ER
428.2
JOH

The Word Wizard's Book of NOUNS

Robin Johnson

Crabtree
Publishing
Company
www.crabtreebooks.com

Word Wizard

Author
Robin Johnson

Publishing plan research and development
Reagan Miller, Crabtree Publishing Company

Editorial director
Kathy Middleton

Project coordinator
Kelly Spence

Editor
Anastasia Suen

Proofreader and indexer
Wendy Scavuzzo

Photo research
Robin Johnson, Katherine Berti

Design & prepress
Katherine Berti

Print coordinator
Katherine Berti

Photographs
All images from Shutterstock

Library and Archives Canada Cataloguing in Publication

Johnson, Robin (Robin R.), author
       The word wizard's book of nouns / Robin Johnson.

(Word wizard)
Includes index.
Issued in print and electronic formats.
ISBN 978-0-7787-1290-9 (bound).--ISBN 978-0-7787-1308-1 (pbk.).--
ISBN 978-1-4271-7760-5 (pdf).--ISBN 978-1-4271-7756-8 (html)

       1. English language--Noun--Juvenile literature. I. Title.

PE1201.J64 2014   j428.2   C2014-903817-8
                                         C2014-903818-6

Library of Congress Cataloging-in-Publication Data

Johnson, Robin (Robin R.) author.
 The Word Wizard's book of nouns / Robin Johnson.
     p. cm. -- (Word Wizard)
 Includes index.
 ISBN 978-0-7787-1290-9 (reinforced library binding) --
 ISBN 978-0-7787-1308-1 (pbk.) -- ISBN 978-1-4271-7760-5 (electronic pdf) --
 ISBN 978-1-4271-7756-8 (electronic html)
 1. English language--Noun--Juvenile literature. 2. English language--Parts
of speech--Juvenile literature. 3. English language--Grammar--Juvenile
literature. I. Title. II. Title: Book of nouns.

 PE1201.J64 2014
 425'.5--dc23
                              2014027801

Crabtree Publishing Company

Printed in the U.S.A./092014/JA20140811

www.crabtreebooks.com   1-800-387-7650

Copyright © **2015 CRABTREE PUBLISHING COMPANY.** All rights reserved. No part of this publication may be reproduced, stored in a retrieval system or be transmitted in any form or by any means, electronic, mechanical, photocopying, recording, or otherwise, without the prior written permission of Crabtree Publishing Company. In Canada: We acknowledge the financial support of the Government of Canada through the Canada Book Fund for our publishing activities.

Published in Canada
Crabtree Publishing
616 Welland Ave.
St. Catharines, Ontario
L2M 5V6

Published in the United States
Crabtree Publishing
PMB 59051
350 Fifth Avenue, 59th Floor
New York, New York 10118

Published in the United Kingdom
Crabtree Publishing
Maritime House
Basin Road North, Hove
BN41 1WR

Published in Australia
Crabtree Publishing
3 Charles Street
Coburg North
VIC 3058

Contents

The magic of words

Words are magical things! They can tell stories without using books. They can paint pictures without brushes. Words can even turn frowns into smiles! Join the Word Wizards in this book. You will see how words work magic!

*You and the Word Wizard will learn the wonder of **nouns**.*

What is the magic word?
They all are!

A world of words

We use words called nouns. Nouns name people, places, and things. We use words to share our ideas. We use words to ask questions. We use words to find answers. What in the world would we do without words?

Word groups

There are all kinds of words! Each word has an important job. Nouns name things. Some words tell how things look. Other words tell how things move. Words are grouped by the jobs they do. Nouns make up one group of words.

ball

girl

piano

cat

brother

game

we

clock

dog

This wizard is in training. He is learning the magic of nouns.

Nouns name

Nouns name people, animals, places, things, or ideas. You are a person. So is the Word Wizard! Wizards pull rabbits out of hats. Rabbits are animals. Hats are things. Wizards make magic in castles. Castles are places. Magic is an idea. You cannot see, hear, smell, taste, or touch idea words. But they are still nouns!

A noun can be as small as a mouse. Or it can be as big as an elephant!

Sentences

We join words together to form **sentences**. Sentences are complete thoughts or ideas. They are made up of nouns and other words. Nouns tell us who or what sentences are about.

Spot the nouns

Every sentence has at least one noun. Some sentences have many nouns. How do you spot nouns? You watch for words that name people, places, animals, things, or ideas.

Word Wizard
in training

Which photo caption has more than one noun? Help the Word Wizard find it! Do the nouns name people, places, animals, things, or ideas?

The farmer works hard.

Cows, pigs, and chickens live on farms.

Singular and plural

A **singular noun** names one person, place, or thing. The word "cookie" is a singular noun. A **plural noun** names more than one person, place, or thing. The word "cookies" is a plural noun. You put cookies in a cookie jar. Then you take a cookie out and eat it!

Making plurals

You do not need magic to make plurals! You just need to add the letter "s." It goes at the end of nouns. Then singular nouns become plural nouns. One cake turns into many cakes. A pie becomes pies. It is as easy as pie!

Word Wizard
in training

Look at these two captions. Which has a plural noun? How can you spot it? Tell the Word Wizard!

This girl has one ice-cream cone.

This boy has three ice-cream cones.

Special rules

Some nouns have special rules. You must add "es" to make them plural. Look at the chart below. It shows which nouns follow this rule.

Noun ends in	Singular nouns	Plural nouns
ch	bunch, witch	bunches, witches
sh	wish, brush	wishes, brushes
s	bus, cactus	buses, cactuses
ss	kiss, mess	kisses, messes
x	fox, box	foxes, boxes
z	waltz, quiz	waltzes, quizzes

These witches are scaring up some fun!

No rules

Other nouns do not follow any rules. They turn into new plural words. It is like a magic trick!

Singular nouns	Plural nouns
person	people
man	men
child	children
woman	women
mouse	mice
foot	feet
tooth	teeth

These mice are nibbling with their teeth.

These children are splashing in bare feet.

Collective nouns

Plural nouns name more than one person, animal, place, thing, or idea. There are also nouns that name groups. They are called **collective nouns**. The word "collective" means shared.

Group work

Some collective nouns name groups of people. Classes and teams are people groups. Other collective nouns name groups of animals. A flock of birds is an animal group. Collective nouns can also name groups of things. A set of dishes is a collective noun. So is a bunch of bananas. What else comes in groups?

Word Wizard in training

Which photo caption has a collective noun? Help the Word Wizard find it!

This family is having fun at a picnic.

These ants are having fun, too!

Possessive nouns

Some nouns end in "s" but are not plurals. They are **possessive nouns**. We use them when a noun **possesses** something. The word "possess" means to have or own. We can say "the toys of the boy." Or we can say "the boy's toys." The word "boy's" is a possessive noun. It shows the toys belong to the boy. Which is easier to understand?

Adding apostrophes

We add an **apostrophe** and "s" to make some nouns possessive. An apostrophe is a mark. It looks like a hook in the air. It grabs the word that the noun owns. For some nouns, we add only an apostrophe—no "s."

Types of nouns	Examples	What you add	Possessive nouns
singular noun that does not end in "s"	father	's	father's
	wizard	's	wizard's
singular noun that ends in "s"	bus	's	bus's
	Tess	's	Tess's
plural noun that does not end in "s"	children	's	children's
	mice	's	mice's
plural noun that ends in "s"	teachers	'	teachers'
	dolls	'	dolls'

Common nouns

Nouns name all kinds of things. Some nouns name everyday things. They name things such as frogs and sandwiches. These words are called **common nouns**. The word "common" means general.

This boy plays basketball every week.

This girl loves her pet hamster.

Proper nouns

We use **proper nouns** to add details. Proper nouns name actual people, places, or things. "Kermit" and "Greenview Public School" are proper nouns. Proper nouns always begin with capital letters. Some are more than one word. Each word begins with a capital letter.

Types of proper nouns	Examples
people	Aunt Kim, Mr. Johnson, Santa Claus
pets and other animals	Fluffy, Whiskers, Slimy
towns, cities, countries, and other places	Nounville, New York, Australia, Canada
calendar words	Tuesday, November
holidays	Christmas, Thanksgiving
products	Granny Lil's Oatmeal Cookies, Frosty's Ice Cream

Pronouns

Some words take the place of nouns. They are called **pronouns**. Pronouns can replace common or proper nouns. They can also replace possessive nouns. We can say, "The teacher tied Sarah's shoes." We can also say, "He tied her shoes." "He" and "hers" are pronouns.

Do not repeat

We use pronouns to make stories interesting. It is boring to repeat the same words. Pronouns do not add details, though. Common nouns give us more information. Proper nouns tell us even more! They help us **communicate**. To communicate means to share ideas.

Word Wizard in training

Look at the two captions. Which sentence has pronouns? Which sentence has proper nouns? Which gives you more information?

The Word Wizard made Willy disappear.

She made him disappear.

Picture it!

Now it is your turn to be a Word Wizard! Grab some paper and crayons. Draw a picture of people or animals. Then write a sentence about them. Use proper nouns in your picture. They will add details to your story.

Get creative!

Add a sun or flowers to your picture. Add a house or car. Add anything you want! Then name all the nouns you see. Are they people, places, animals, things, or ideas?

Work your magic! Turn a blank page into a noun cartoon!

Learning more

Books

A Lime, a Mime, a Pool of Slime: More about Nouns (Words Are CATegorical) by Brian P. Cleary. Millbrook Press, 2008.

A Pocket Full of Nouns (Words I Know) by Bette Blaisdell. A+ Books, 2014.

If You Were a Noun (Word Fun) by Michael Dahl. Nonfiction Picture Books, 2006.

Nouns (Grammar Basics) by Kate Riggs. Creative Paperbacks, 2013.

Nouns (Language Rules!) by Ann Heinrichs. Child's World, 2010.

Websites

Visit this website for noun games, activities, jokes, and quizzes.
www.brainpopjr.com/readingandwriting/word/nouns

This website has noun lessons, games, quizzes, and pages to print.
www.anglomaniacy.pl/grammar-nouns.htm

Learn more about nouns with these videos, quizzes, and games.
www.grammaropolis.com/noun.php

Shoot some hoops and learn about nouns at this web page.
www.harcourtschool.com/activity/basketball/index_pre.html

Words to know

apostrophe (uh-POS-truh-fee) A mark used to show that a noun owns something

collective noun (kuh-LEK-tiv nown) A word that names a group of people, animals, or things

common noun (KOM-uhn nown) A noun that names a general person, place, animal, thing, or idea

communicate (kuh-MYOO-ni-keyt) To share ideas and information

noun (nown) A word that names a person, animal, place, thing, or idea

plural noun (PLOOR-uhl nown) A word that names more than one person, animal, place, thing, or idea

possess (puh-ZES) To have or to own

possessive noun (puh-ZES-iv nown) A word that shows a noun has or owns something

pronoun (PROH-nown) A word that takes the place of a noun

proper noun (PROP-er nown) A word that names an actual person, place, animal, thing, or idea

sentence (SEN-tns) A complete thought or idea

singular noun (SING-gyuh-ler nown) A word that names one person, animal, place, thing, or idea

Index